Let's Learn More About
Eid al-Adha

Seven Sabeels Press

Assalamualaikum,
May peace be upon you.
If you and your children enjoyed
this book and found it beneficial,
please help us to leave a review.
Thank you!

Written by: Sheila Ibrahim
Illustrated by: Filza Amalina

ISBN: 9798529421987

Early one morning, Yusuf returned home from the mosque with his family.

Emma, his neighbor, was outside playing with her new toy airplane.

"Yusuf, do you want to play too?"

"I'm sorry, but I can't," he said. "I'm wearing my new Eid clothes."

"What's Eid?" Emma asked.

"Eid al-Adha is an Islamic holiday," Yusuf explained. "We wake up early and go to the mosque to pray. Then we come back home, and...well, why don't you come celebrate with us and see?"

Emma was curious, so she followed Yusuf's family into their home.

The house was nicely decorated, and there were plenty of sweet treats on the table. Yusuf invited Emma to try some as he prepared to color.

Emma pointed to a picture. "What's this?" she asked.

"It's the Kaaba," Yusuf answered. "It's located in Mecca and it's also the direction Muslims face when they pray."

"What does it have to do with Eid al-Adha?"

"Eid al-Adha occurs during the final days of the Hajj. It's a holy pilgrimage where Muslims travel to see the Kaaba and do different acts of worship, like pray together."

"Yusuf!" his mother called, "please help me pack up the food."

Emma followed Yusuf into the kitchen. There were food and uncooked

meat everywhere. "What's all this for?" she wondered aloud.

"One-third of the meat is for us to keep, one-third to share, and one-

third to give to those in need," Yusuf's mother replied.

"On Eid al-Adha," Yusuf's mother explained, "Prophet Ibrahim was instructed by God to sacrifice his son. Of course, Prophet Ibrahim loved his son very much but he decided to do as he was told. Little did he knew, God only wanted to test Prophet Ibrahim's faith. So, God rewarded his obedience by giving him a ram to sacrifice instead."

The meat and food were all packed, and Emma was bursting with excitement. She could not wait to help!

They began to walk through the neighborhood and stopped at the first house.

"Is the family here Muslim too?" Emma asked.

"No," Yusuf said. "We help anyone in need, both Muslim and non-Muslim."

As they knocked on doors, Emma observed that people would smile and say "Eid Mubarak" to each other.

"What does 'Eid Mubarak' mean?" she asked.

Yusuf smiled. "It means 'Happy Eid!'"

When they reached the last house, Emma noticed a boy looking at her toy airplane. She remembered the story of Prophet Ibrahim's sacrifice. Her new toy was important to her. But many people — like Prophet Ibrahim — made important sacrifices too.

Emma marched to the door and held out her toy. "Eid Mubarak!" she

proudly said.

"Eid Mubarak!" The boy gladly accepted the toy airplane. "Thank you!"

"You're welcome!" Emma felt good inside. She liked how she felt after

helping others.

"I feel very happy," she told Yusuf. "I know now that Eid al-Adha is about showing kindness and making others happy, too."

"And giving them what they need, even if it's what you want," he said.

"And cooking lots of delicious food!" she giggled.

"And strengthening ties with the community and your loved ones,"
Yusuf's mom added. "Like we will soon do when Uncle Hassan and his
family come to visit."

On the way back home, Emma reflected on her little act of sacrifice and looked forward to celebrating Eid al-Adha again. "Next year, though," she thought, "I'll make sure to have gifts ready!"

Glossary

- Prophet Ibrahim (ee-bruh-heem): Also known as Abraham in the Bible, Prophet Ibrahim is a prophet and a messenger of God in Islam.

- Kaaba: A cube-shaped building in Mecca that is considered by Muslims to be the most sacred site in the world. Muslims worldwide face the direction of the Kaaba when they pray.

- Hajj: An annual Islamic pilgrimage to Mecca located in Saudi Arabia that Muslims are expected to make once in their lifetime if they can afford it and are physically fit.

- Eid Mubarak: A phrase to wish someone a happy or blessed Eid.

- Eid al-Adha: Also known as Feast of the Sacrifice, Eid al-Adha is the day where Muslims commemorate Prophet Ibrahim's test of faith and are reminded to be steadfast in their obedience to God.

Summary

- Morning congregational Eid prayer

Muslims usually perform the Eid morning prayer at the mosque or in open outdoor spaces. After the prayer, the Imam (the prayer leader) will deliver a sermon.

- Hajj

Eid al-Adha coincides with the last days of the Hajj. While Muslims worldwide celebrate the Islamic holiday, millions of pilgrims carry out the final days of Hajj in Mecca, Saudi Arabia.

- Wearing clean and new outfits

For those who can afford it, it's especially recommended to wear a clean and new outfit to celebrate the joyous occasion.

- Having delicious meals and sweet treats

Delicious meals and sweet treats are often served on the day of Eid al-Adha to celebrate the joyous occasion.

Summary

- Sacrificing an animal

Muslims who have the financial means would purchase an animal, usually a goat, cow, or sheep, in order for it to be sacrificed. One-third of the meat is to be cooked at home, one-third is to be shared with relatives and friends, and one-third is to be given to the poor in charity.

- Helping those who are less fortunate

One-third of the sacrificed meat is distributed to the poor and less fortunate. Money and items can also be donated as a form of charity.

- Visiting relatives & exchanging gifts

Eid is also about spending time with relatives and loved ones. On Eid al-Adha, Muslims visit the homes of their relatives and may exchange gifts too. The most common practice is to gift money to younger relatives.

Made in United States
North Haven, CT
26 April 2022

18629556R00020